The Tortoise and the Rabbit

Retold by Jeffery L. Williams

Illustrated by Alessandro Pastori

Once upon a time, there was a race to see which animal was faster.

Tortoise and Rabbit were friends. They each wanted to win.

"I can win this race!" said Rabbit. "I do everything quickly. I won't have to try very hard."
Then he said to Tortoise, "You do everything slowly. You won't win this race!"

"I can win this race!" said Tortoise. "I do everything slowly. So I will have to try very hard."

The next morning, Rabbit ate his breakfast quickly. He *did not* try hard to tie his shoes.

Tortoise ate his breakfast slowly. He *did* try hard and tied his shoes well.

"Ready! Set! Go!"

Rabbit ran quickly and his shoes came off.
"I have time to stop to look for them," he said.
So he did. But Tortoise went on slowly.

Then Rabbit got hungry. "I have time to stop and eat something," he said. So he did. But Tortoise went on slowly.

"I am tired from looking for my shoes and eating. I have time to stop and take a nap," said Rabbit. So he did.

But Tortoise went on slowly.

Rabbit woke up and ran quickly to the finish line.

But when he got there, Tortoise had won the race.

"I guess going slow and trying hard *can* win the race," said Rabbit.